30 Best Real Estate Investing Strategies for Beginner Real Estate Investors

Michael Joshua

DEDICATION

I would like to dedicate this book to all the first time real estate investors out there. May your journey through finding the right real estate to invest in be a fun adventure and not a stressful one. May the financial aspect of it be rewarding and not a burden.

DISCLAIMER

No part of this eBook can be transmitted or reproduced in any form
including print, electronic, photocopying, scanning, mechanical or
recording devices without prior written permission from the author.

CONTENTS

CHAPTER 1: INTRODUCTION TO REAL ESTATE INVESTMENTS

Real estate investment comprise of sale or/and rental, management, ownership, and purchase of real estate properties for profit. Realty property improvement as a part of investment strategy of real estate is usually considered as a sub-specialty of real estate investing, known as real estate development.

Real estate investing is defined as the real estate which creates income or is intended for investment purposes instead of primary residence. Real estate investors own various real estate properties, of which one is their residential property while the rest are utilized for generating profits and rental income via price appreciation.

It is rather a lucrative business but if the factors or basics of this business aren't managed or understood well by the investor, it can result in massive losses. However, with proper knowledge, understanding, as well as the right strategies, you can end up being a millionaire in just a few years.

Why Real Estate?

Even though, real estate may not be a golden ticket for many, it still is a rather stable investment not only in for short term but also for long term. Whilst other investment avenues may be witnessing a bad slide, real estate investment is continually witnessing gains.

People owning a home and buying another one solely for the purpose of renting can enjoy capital gains. Not only this, but the mortgage pays for itself as the rent being paid by the tenants.

As the federal government started tracking the figure from 30 years ago, it is determined that the prices of average homes are yet to see a year-over-year decline. A few metropolitan markets have experienced certain downfalls which affected the investors but aside from those rare cases, the real estate profit forecast has been constantly rosy.

For most of the people, the demands and efforts of long term commitments like owning a real estate might appear too massive to ignore but if one goes through the benefits, a few sacrifices can effectively be made in order to achieve more benefits in the future.

The real estate investment even comes through in the short term. For instance, if the value of your property is fairly cheap, you can invest in its renovations and then sell the house. The value of the house will drastically increase due to the renovations.

Investing in real estate is the decision many individuals make at one point of their life, in hopes of earning wealth. Even though, there are plenty of investment options like cash, bonds, and stocks, real estate investments appears to be one of the easiest and safest option.

Advantages of Real Estate Investing

Here are few of the many benefits of real estate investing:

Capital Growth

Overtime, the property value will increase and would prove to be financially beneficial for you. Not only will you enjoy a fixed capital growth but will also benefit from the monthly rental returns.

A Safe Investment

Real estate investment is the only market which isn't dominated by investors; this has created a natural buffer in the market. Not only is this safe, but is also a forgiving investment – meaning, if you buy one of the worst properties in a certain area, there are high chances that its value will increase in the future.

Mitigate Risk

Your asset can be insured against a majority of the risks, including property damage, fire damage, or tenant breaking the lease or leaving.

Anyone can Invest

There isn't a need for massive knowledge in this market as you may need with stocks or for investing in a business.

Control

You have complete control over your real estate investment, unlike other investment options. You are the one making decisions and have control over the returns.

Tax Benefits

Even though the tax benefits shouldn't be utilized as a major factor in the decision making, it is a good benefit of real estate investing.

What Makes Up A Good Investment Property?

A well selected property is most probable to provide better return to you in the future, not merely in the form of steady capital growth but in rental returns as well. To ensure that you maximize your returns from investments, here are a few things to consider:

Right Property Cycle Stage

It is essential to understand that the real estate market moves in cycles. The value of the properties might increase because of a strong growth in the market, might stay steady, or might decrease in value during different phases of the cycle. Therefore, it is important for an investor to have knowledge about the real estate cycle to make sure that the property is secured at the best price.

Right Location

Location of the property is another essential element to consider when selecting an investment property. If you select the correct location, there will be high chances that you will gain high returns through your investment. In contrast, selecting a property at an unsuitable or less desired location might not give you as high return as you expected.

Here are a few factors to consider when selecting the location of your property:

- Should be in close proximity of main amenities as it enhances the value and desirability of the property. These amenities may include:
  - Lifestyle activities (beach, cafés, restaurants, malls, etc.)
  - Markets and shops
  - Public facilities (medical centers, parks, libraries, post offices, etc.)
  - Public transportation
  - Schools
- When choosing a location, it is best to avoid the ones that are dependent on a single industry i.e. manufacturing. However, it might be beneficial if that industry is flourishing but if it falls, so will the value of your property.
- The best locations to purchase a property at are the ones that are going through a population growth. As

the population increases, there is an improvement in the infrastructure and the desirability of that location grows as well.

- People prefer living close to a major city. Whilst various suburbs attract high prices, opt for the one that has potentially strong population growth.

The Right Property

When looking for an investment property, it is best to aim for the one which will be in high demands by both the tenants and home buyers. Consider the property's appropriateness for average age of the individuals living in the locality.

It is significant to do some research regarding the demographics of the location you are interested in buying and also to understand what is more important for that demographic. For instance, when purchasing a property in an area with an older community, avoid buying the one with an inconvenient layout or a staircase.

The Right Return

Majority of the real estate investors make a grave mistake of selecting the property on the basis of emotion, instead of logic and finances. A bad buy might lead to a capital growth which would be below the average market value or rental income.

This won't even come near in covering the monthly expenses of maintaining the property. Therefore, it is important to research in order to come up with the right strategy before you make the purchase.

The Property Cycle Explained

It is a known fact that the property market moves in cycles. As mentioned before, the value rises with a growth in the market, stays constant, or decline with a decrease in the market growth. Ultimately, however, the property's value grows over time.

There are different phases of the property cycle and you must invest before considering which phase the market is in currently. Following are the four phases of the property cycle:

The Boom Phase

This is the shortest phase of the cycle. In this phase, the value of the property increases rapidly. It starts slow as the real estate investors realize that the returns of property, like property prices and rental payments, are increasing.

Due to this boom, properties are sold for a lot higher than their original asking price, as buyers start competing with one another and sellers continue pushing the prices up.

During the boom, most of the investors want to get on board and make the most of it. New investors join in while the existing home owners, builders, as well as developers flood the market with numerous properties. Gradually, this results in excess supply which then leads to the end of the boom phase and the market enters the slump phase.

The Slump Phase

When the market gets flooded with properties, this oversupply leads the market towards the slump phase. With an increased number of investment properties in the market, the rate of vacancies rises and the rental returns start decreasing.

In this phase, the prices stop increases and may even start declining in certain cases. Majority of new home buyers start struggling with repayments during this stage as most of the buyers overcommit themselves whilst in boom stage by buying real estate which they can't afford and when the interest rates increase, it gets difficult for them to make the repayments.

Hence, the only solution for them is to sell the property to get themselves out of this financial issue, and mostly, they have to sell at decreased prices.

The Stabilization Phase

Usually, the real estate market doesn't jump from a bad period to an upturn one. A short phase exists between the phases where the market starts to stabilize as the economic factors start catching up with one another.

The Upturn Phase

In this phase, the rate of vacancies starts to fall, rents start to increase and the value of real estate starts to rise which creates investment opportunities. The values of the properties typical increases in the inner suburbs or the ones near the beach first. Afterwards, starts increasing in the middle ring of the suburbs and gradually to the outer parts of the suburbs.

At the middle of this phase, real estate properties are usually affordable and the property investment returns are favorable. The value start increasing gradually and peak in the boom phase. However, the favorable conditions in the upturn phase attracts numerous investors and home buyers which gradually push the cycle in its next boom phase. The cycle then repeats.

Tax for Property Investors

Real estate investment offers buyers the luxury of specific tax benefits. However, you may also incur extra taxes as an investor. Following is a simple breakdown of the taxes linked with property investment:

Tax Incurred

There are various taxes which an investor must incur when owning and acquiring an investment property, including:

Income Tax

You would have to taxes on the income, including rent or other money, which you earn through your property. However, this might be offset through interest repayment on your loans and other deductions.

Capital Gains Tax (CGT)

The CGT must be paid on the profits you have made through your investment properties when they are sold. The CGT's applicable rate is similar to the rate of income tax you pay. However, if the property was owned by you for more than 12 months then you get a 50% discount on the capital gain.

Property Taxes

This is also known as council rate and is a local tax which usually funds the local government expenditure and investment like public and park facility maintenance, garbage collection, and other community services. The amount and frequency of the tax amount depends on the property's market value and the local municipality.

Land Tax

Land tax is enforced by every territory and state government. It is payable on the basis of your property's combined unimproved value and is estimated on what the value of your land would be if vacant. This is why it doesn't include the property's existing dwellings. This tax is payable on all properties you own, excluding your residence. The amount usually varies according to locality.

The Deductions

There are three expense categories which the investors have the luxury to deduct from the taxes. These are:

Acquisition and Maintenance Costs

The expenses related to your investment property can be offset against rental income, whether it was or wasn't negatively geared. A few of the expenses that you, as an investor, can claim are:

- Water charges
- Expenses for the maintenance or inspection of your property
- Car and travel expenses for inspections or rent collection

- Tax-related expenses
- Postage and stationery expenses
- Maintenance and repairs
- Surveyors' fees
- Gas and electricity bills not paid by the tenant
- Property manager commissions and fees
- Legal expenses
- Land tax
- Investment loans interest
- Insurance – landlord, building, etc.
- Investment related telephone bills
- Council rates
- Cleaning costs
- Body corporate fees
- Borrowing expenses
- Bank charges and fees on loan accounts
- Advertising costs to attract tenants

Depreciation Allowances

Every landlord owning an investment property is eligible for claiming depreciation on all the new purchased items. The depreciation can be deducted on fittings and fixtures in the property, like:

- Hot water system
- Furniture
- Carpets
- Blinds
- Appliances

Negative Gearing

This happens when yearly investment cost is higher as

compared to the return you receive. In other words, when the ongoing expenses like loan repayments and maintenance are higher as compared to rental income then it means that the property is negatively geared. If this happens to an investor, the government permits the property loss to be deducted from the gross income which creates a decrease in the tax liability.

CHAPTER 2: 30 BEST STRATEGIES FOR REAL ESTATE INVESTING

Real estate is a unique investment and the typical rules applied in investing bonds and stocks, can't be applied here. In order to become a successful real estate investor, it is essential to understand various strategies and learn when and where to apply them.

This chapter highlights the 30 best strategies for real estate investing which could help you become a millionaire eventually.

1. *Residential Property*

Majority individual begin their real estate investing career from the residential sector for two major reasons. Many people have a good knowledge and understanding about the working of the residential sector.

This decreases the learning curve dramatically. So, as you are a beginner, you can start from this strategy. Remember, residential investing is a rather different than owning your own home. This strategy is ideal because the cost is a lot lower as compared to other sectors and the entry barrier is also low. There are good chances that you will succeed and earn a decent amount of cash.

2. Commercial Property

Commercial real estate is typically more profitable as compared to real estate. One would obviously pay more for a shop in a mall than for a duplex or single house. You will have an increased amount of income stream every month.

Furthermore, business make a multiyear lease instead of an annual lease which usually happens in residential properties. When the business earns success at your commercial property, they are most likely to stay for good. Majority of such businesses stay for years which means you will have a steady monthly income.

There are several strategies that you can apply in both commercial and residential property as well like buying multiple ones to create various income streams. You can keep a look out for the ones that perform the best and sell off the ones that deliver the least profit.

This way you can reinvest that money on some other profitable property. It is essential for you to select a niche first, for instance a retail place, manufacturing space, or a hotel.

3. Buy and Hold

This is the most common and most popular strategy in real estate investing. It means buying a property and renting it for a prolong time. Buy and hold is a simplest and purest strategy of real estate investing.

As a beginner investor, you will gain your wealth by buying a property and then either holding it to sell it for a profit in the future or rent it out and collect monthly income. The benefits of this strategy is that when you are holding a property and renting it out, the mortgage gets paid down monthly which reduces the principle balance and enhances your property's equity.

One major thing for buy and hold investor is understanding and learning the ways of evaluating opportunities and deals. The most common mistake made by many investors in this strategy is purchasing bad deals because they don't properly understand the property evaluation.

Another mistake commonly made is underestimation of expenses, bad decisions on selection of tenants, and not managing it properly.

All of this can be avoided if you learn the basics first instead of simply jumping in the business.

In order to effectively use this strategy, you must understand the ways of identifying the ebb and flow of the market in which the property is located in. Once the investors determine that the properties they are interested in are at low point (high inventory, low prices), they buy the property.

Once the market begins to overheat, a good buy and hold investor would cease from buying any more properties till things start settling down. Throughout these low phases, investors might sell or just hold their properties.

A few buy and sell investors don't sell their properties and prefer to have their mortgage paid off through the monthly cash flow or might opt to sell the property via 'seller financing'.

4. Flipping

One great strategy of earning more money through real estate is flipping houses, the popularity is mostly because of its promotions on various cable TV shows. This is the practice of purchasing a property at a low price, making improvements in it, and then selling it for a profit.

Basically, house flipping is rather similar to 'buy low, sell high' factor in majority of the retail businesses.

A common kind of property which gets flip is a single family home. A real estate investor follows the rule of thumb called the 70% rule, and purchases a house for 70% of its existing value.

For instance, a house should be valued at $100,000 but requires $20,000 work on it. A house flipper will buy it for $50,000 and try selling it for $100,000 once the work is completed.

This is merely a rule of thumb and values should be adjusted and verified to make sure that the flip is profitable and successful.

One major element of house flipping is speed. If you want to flip house successfully, you will have to purchase the property, have it improved, and sell it as fast as you can to gain maximum profit and to save yourself from months of carrying costs.

The carrying costs comprise of property taxes, financing charges, utilities, condo fees, and other maintenance expenses need to ensure that the house is in good financial standing.

Flipping houses is an active job not a passive task. Once you stop flipping, you will stop earning money till you start it again.

5. Wholesaling

Wholesaling is a strategy in which the investor finds good real estate deals, write a contract to get that deal, and sell that contract to other buyer. In general, a wholesaler doesn't own a property they sell but merely look for different deals via marketing strategies, put them in contract, and then sell it off for a specific fee.

The usual fee they charge on average is between $500 and $5,000 or may be even more as per the deal's size.

A few investors prefer selling the contracts to retail buyers but majority of them sell them out to other investors (usually house flippers), who usually are cash buyers. When a wholesaler deals with these cash buyers, they typically get paid in a few days or within a week. This also enables them to create strong connections in the real estate community.

Most of the new real estate investors start with wholesaling because of it being a simple and easy strategy with low cost of startup. As the wholesaler doesn't actually own the property, there aren't any loan fees, rehab costs, banks, tenants, contractors, and other such complications.

This makes the wholesaling strategy popular among real estate investors. However, it isn't that easy to become a successful retailer as it sounds.

It is essential for the wholesalers to continuously seek out different deals to create an inventory from which they can sell to others. They must also have an effective marketing strategy to attract buyers.

This strategy is mostly promoted as the one which anyone can do, even those with no money. However, you would ultimately need some financial resources to create your marketing funnel.

Aside from that, the investors persisting in enhancing their wholesaling abilities usually gain success and end up with a stable income source as they grow their knowledge of other successful strategies.

6. Rehabs

There are plenty of opportunities to rehab; you simply must know the places to look. It is undoubtedly one of the best real estate strategies available. Rehabbing is rather popular and is usually used by majority of the real estate investors.

Rehabbing means purchasing properties in a decreased price

and selling it for a profit by making certain upgrades first. Single family houses are the main target for real estate investors as they offer most appealing spreads for the required amount of work.

Although, rehabs is the most work intensive strategy, the rewards through this strategy are completely worth it. It offers the real estate investors with the biggest spreads in a short time. You should consider the rehabbing strategy if the following conditions have been met:

- There is a strong team you trust who can work on the property, including title company, lenders, contractors etc.
- The property is located at a prime and safe location
- There is a greater possibility of a big profit margin
- You are determined to generate brand awareness
- You don't require immediate payment

7. Short Sales

Once a while, there is an individual who discovers a means of owing more on the property as compared to the worth of the property. This is usually accomplished by a mixture of interest-only mortgage, second mortgages, home equity loans, and some other liens against the property.

For instance, your property is worth $200,000 but you owe $215,000, you won't be able to find anyone who would pay $215,000 nor would any agent sell that property as they won't earn any commission on it. The only strategies left for that individual are either a foreclosure or a short sale investor.

In such situation, the bank would be the only one who would want this property less than you. This is because taking a foreclosed house means the bank loses abundance of lending powers.

This is where you, as a short sale investor, comes in. A short sale investor is well qualified to talk to lenders, banks, and anyone else who require money from the property owner. These investors explain to all the involved people about how the house would go for foreclosure and to get any money, they would have to settle for less instead of the full amount.

A short sale investor helps the owner in paying everyone they owe less amount then the actual outstanding cost. After this, the house which was $15,000 in negative can be bought for a low cost by the investor instead of getting foreclosed.

8. Subject To/Lease Options

Here is a creative strategy that a real estate investor can use. Let's assume, there is someone who is struggling to sell their house, and it has been several months since the house has been on the market. The house owner really wants to get rid of it. You, as an investor, offer to buy their house – not immediately, but in a few years.

With this, you also offer to make their monthly mortgage payments will you purchase the house. On top of this, you also give them a few thousand dollars upfront. This would sound fine for the house owner but how would you earn money through this?

You would ask the owners to move out and would find another party to move in. This party isn't looking to rent the house but wants to buy one. This is referred as lease option buyer.

Instead of immediately buying the house, the potential buyer will live in that house for up to a year and then would make the decision of either buying the house or not. This is a best option for the buyers who want to buy a house but want to first experience the neighborhood or the house or they need a little time to improve their credits or any other reason why they aren't able to immediately buy a house.

This is how the money would be made – when a potential buyer starts living in the house with an option of buying it after a year, it cost some money. You, as an investor, can hand a certain amount of money to the actual home owner who has moved out and keep the rest for yourself.

Lease option buyers have to pay a little more as compared to the regular renters. For instance, if the lease option buyer is paying you $1,200 monthly and the mortgage is $1,000 monthly then you would be able to pay the mortgage and keep $200 for yourself.

Lastly, once you offer to purchase the house in a few months, you would set the price at the existing market value, for instance $200,000. When the lease option buyer decides to buy the house after a year, the price will be set at the market value at that time.

The value of the house is bound to have increased by $10,000 - $50,000 or even more. So, the value of the house might increase to $230,000 after a year. The lease option buyer will purchase the house at $230,000; you will pay the actual house owner $200,000 and would earn $30,000 from this deal.

In case, the lease option buyer doesn't buy the house after a year, you can simply find another potential buyer. You can then collect a lease option fees, make a certain amount of money every month, and then get two years' worth of increased house value instead of one in the end.

9. Land Development/Construction

How can you make money with land? Wait till the value of the land goes up, or make a few improvements on the land to increase its value. This is another great real estate investing strategy as land construction or development brings with it various options one can opt for.

One great way of making more money is by subdividing the land into various different housing lots or commercial buildings. This is a surefire way of boosting the value of that land. If the land has plumbing, electricity, and roads then the worth of the land would go up even more. Creating just a single building on that land can also increase its value.

Another good tactic would be to subdivide the land, sell half or some part of it, and construct houses or commercial buildings on the remaining parts with the money you receive. You can also sell off some of those buildings and houses to pay for improvements of the remaining buildings or construction of the new ones.

In the end, you will have a piece of property on a well developed land which started from just a piece of bare land.

Although land construction and development typically take years to finish but investors earn millions in the end.

10. Creative Real Estate Deals

One thing that must be understood is that there are limitless possibilities in real estate investing. It doesn't matter that you have little knowledge, have bad credit, have limited time, or are short on cash.

You merely have to focus on what you already have, and seek individuals who can add what you lack. This is known as leverage, which means you utilize the skills, knowledge, money, and time of other individuals to make money for yourself.

For example, an investor found that an apartment complex valued at $800 was available at $600. When he passes this information to a more experienced investor, he would receive $50K.

There isn't even a need to make a strategy when you have network of professional investors you can pass on the deals to and earn a certain bit of cash simply for passing on information.

You will find many such creative ways and strategies to earn good money in real estate investing. Another creative strategy is to buy run down houses in locations which are expected to go through significant appreciation.

Since you don't have to pay capital gains tax if you have lived in a house for more than two years, you can buy a rundown house, spend two years to fix it up, and then sell it for more than $100K for all the improvement and appreciation you put in it. Repeat the same procedure to earn more money.

There are many beginner investors who aren't aware about the fact that they can utilize IRA's and 401K's to real estate investing. There is sufficient cash that simply sit in underperforming mutual funds, so if you can offer people a higher return as compared to stock market then you can combine the accounts of various people to fund your real estate deals.

Once you start learning about real estate investing and spend more time with experienced investors, you will learn that there are plenty of creative ways through which you can utilize your own as well as other people's resources to make them and yourself wealthy.

11. Building & Developing

This strategy is gaining plenty of attention lately. From the development of apartment buildings to single family rentals, there are numerous options in this niche. Although this strategy is rather exciting, it can be risky and is more financially demanding as compared to other options.

There are numerous factors involved in this strategy including project approval, market analysis, land location, and many decision making processes to make this strategy a success. As an investor, it is essential for you to learn about the project's viability for potential marketability and profitability.

You must learn to evaluate the property to determine its best and highest usage, understand the process of building and development, know how to distinguish the disadvantages and advantages of the property, find the right partners and right amount of cash when necessary, and understand the importance and relevance of option agreements and contracts.

12. *Private Lending*

Although it may appear a little unorthodox to approach the real estate investing industry from the private money lending perspective, but it is not so in reality. In fact, many successful real estate investors aspire to become private money lenders.

The interest rates on traditional institutions are expected to increase which means more and more investors are making their way in providing services of private lending. Typically, private mortgage lending has provided 8% to 10% of annual return based on historical rates of interests charged to borrowers.

This means you can earn plenty of money through this strategy. Other benefits of private lending include:

- Minimal Volatility
- Diversification
- Capital Preservation
- Reliable Cash Flow

13. Mortgage Notes

Individuals who have the necessary capital but want to avoid the headache and hassle related to hands-on management can opt for mortgage notes. This strategy will enable you to enjoy the resultant cash while the heavy lifting is done by others for you.

14. Partnerships

Partnerships in real estate have been around for ages. The main reason is that investors have learned to pool together their resources to minimize the risks and enhance the leverages. A partnership helps the investors to have a bigger down payment, greater experience, or stronger financial statements by pooling resources.

Today, there are various types of partnerships in the real estate investment arena. You have the option of investing in REIT (Real Estate Investment Trust), a TIC (Tenant In Common) project, with business partners, in separate LLP (Limited Liability Partnership), or as LLC (Limited Liability Corporation).

The partnership can be fully benefit from when all partners have similar investment goals, are experienced, aren't dependent on income, and have invested some time in planning out a good partnership structure.

To work with a partner or two in real estate investing is always prudent and is even a necessity in some cases. This is a particularly good option for investors who are just starting out as having a partner assists in offsetting the risk of even a small amount of investment.

Even experienced investors prefer to take on partners for the very same reason because as they deal with bigger deals, the risks are greater as well. Furthermore, individual real estate investors also benefit from the diverse perspectives, experience, and wisdom which other partners can offer.

Two major advantages of the many that partnerships offer are indeed pooling resources and double analysis. Investing may require plenty of resources, typically lotto many for a single individual to handle on their own.

However, if you partner with an individual with similar work ethics, goals, and interests then you both can pool your resources to get off to a smooth start. This helps in protecting your assets and decreasing the risks.

Aside from that, it also helps in analyzing the deals in a better manner. This is especially true for beginner investors who have yet to learn and experience proper analysis the property. When you have a partner with you, it can help in double analysis of the deal to ensure there aren't any risks that you failed to identify.

There are plenty of considerations when looking for a deal, so having someone to double check your analysis enhances the possibility of ending up with a more accurate analysis. This can also save you from potential disasters and losses.

15. Core

The Core strategy is the least risky one in real estate investment but also offers low returns on the low risks. A good example of core investment is investing in a high rise apartment building which is fully stabilized but has a low vacancy rate.

16. Core-Plus

Core plus investing strategy means investing in a property which requires some remodeling, repairs, tenant retention, or other necessary additions in order to enhance the property value for it to have an acceptable return rate. This strategy has comparatively more risk than core investing strategy because of the required additional enhancements.

17. Value Add

This investing strategy means investing in a property that requires more work than simply a few repairs. It also focuses on other factors like mechanical or physical and management needs, and cash flow.

18. Opportunistic

This strategy is considered a high risk one but also leads to much higher returns. Opportunistic investing is investment in those properties which require drastic rehabilitation and improvements, including new constructions.

19. *Seller Financing*

Seller financing means selling a property to a buyer but carrying on the mortgage rather than asking the buyer to get their own. Numerous real estate investors from around the globe opt for this strategy for many reasons.

During a normal sale, the buyer seeks the bank's assistance in obtaining financing for the house and the seller gets the complete sale price. However, with seller financing, the seller becomes the bank who assists the buyer in financing the house.

The buyer provides the down payment to the seller and also pays the mortgage payments monthly till the buyers decides to sell the house or till the life of the loan.

This strategy is utilized for various reasons but mostly for buyers who don't qualify for normal mortgage. The existing lending environment makes it difficult for the various buyers to get traditional financing for their houses.

This might be for many reasons including bad credit score, self-employment, or they might not be able to document all of the income.

However, it is important to understand that seller financing isn't only for benefiting buyers who don't qualify for mortgage. Majority of the investors opt for selling their properties via seller financing strategy to get a steady monthly income which doesn't include rentals, tenants, or maintenance.

Once the property is sold off through seller financing, the new buyer is 100% responsible for the property which means all rights, as well as expenses, must be handled by the new buyer including cost of maintenance, insurance, and taxes.

An investor might also opt for this strategy to offset the due taxes at the end of their investing career because the IRS classifies it as 'installment sale' and permits the investor to spread out all the capital tax gains which might be due.

20. Tax Lien Certificates

Guaranteed by government and secured by real estate, these tax-defaulted papers are an effective strategy being utilized by successful investors for decades. Other delinquent taxes in return for a high interest rate, and in some cases, getting the property itself, make this a useful strategy for many investors.

However, it is essential for you to understand the difference between tax deeds and tax lien certificates, ways of researching properties, as well as determining the risk factors involved in the process. Here are a few things you must consider when opting for this strategy:

- Exploring online auctions to get the best deals
- Learning ways to use the excess proceeds
- Understanding systems and processes of acquiring tax delinquent properties

- Educating yourself about the basics of tax foreclosure investing.

21. Foreclosures

Foreclosed properties can be acquired via two different methods – bank REOs and actions. It is essential to understand that you need to make proper preparations before you make a bid at an auction.

It is recommended that you become a major participant in the auctioning process and learn ways of finding and approaching the banks to acquire REOs. Furthermore, you will also need to learn about property lists and how to effectively use them. You should learn to analyze a deal effectively and identify the main elements of the REO offer.

22. Probate Purchases

A probate property is the one which is owned by a deceased individual. When an owner of a house dies, two things happen – either the property is handed to the heir of the deceased or there isn't any will or heir to pass down the property to.

In case the property is passed down to the heir, the real estate investors still may have an opportunity of purchasing the property as in many cases the heir of the deceased view the property as a burden on them since they already have a good place to live and would be relieved to get rid of it in order to avoid the costs of insurance, taxes, and maintenance.

However, in case there isn't any will or heir of the deceased, the property goes to the probate court to be sold off. The state becomes the in charge of selling that house.

They usually sell it for the highest price but the value of that house is still below the value in the market. This is a great opportunity, especially for the flippers to purchase a valuable property at a cheaper cost.

Probate purchase strategy is the most profitable strategy in the real estate investing market. This reason is that there isn't much competition since it is extremely hard to find the leads and it also takes plenty of time in the courthouse.

Once the investor gets hold of the property, the next thing they do is get it repaired and sell it off at a good price. It is important to understand that there are various probate laws that differ from state to state and you must have adequate knowledge about the right way of making probate sales.

23. Subject-To Purchases

The subject to purchases means *"subject to existing mortgage"* on the property. It means that you would be making the remaining payments on behalf of the original owner. Before you opt for this strategy, it is important to properly analyze the property, existing financing, the market, as well as the seller.

Furthermore, it is also essential to have a written contract between you and the owner, which clearly states all the terms you both have agreed upon.

24. Owner-Financed Notes

You can make significant passive income when you purchase secured owner financed notes. Investors must learn the art of negotiation to purchase, structure, and create the notes.

There is due diligence required in verifying and compiling required information, calculating the offer, and analyzing the risk factors of the deal. You must also fully understand the process of funding and closing the note purchase transaction thoroughly.

25. IRA and Retirement Plan Investing

The advantages of utilizing IRA as a strategy offer the investors a freedom to invest in what they want, instead of what their stockbroker or insurance company offers. The first thing you need to do is to learn about self-directed retirement plans and ways of utilizing them to make a real estate investment.

It is also essential to understand the prohibited transactions and how you can avoid them. Successful investors explore different techniques and principles to properly manage the entire process.

26. Fix and Flip

This is a great strategy to earn good money. The main challenge in this strategy is that you have to find a property cheap enough that can earn you a profit once you are done fixing it. Once you find a property at a cheap price, you must make all the repairs as soon as you can and sell of the property quickly.

You have to be careful about paying too much for the repairs or underestimating the cost of repairs, as this can cost you more money than you had estimated and this strategy won't work for you.

27. Prehabbing

Prehabbing is considered as a prelude to rehabbing. It might also refer to light and simpler rehabbing. This strategy has started becoming more popular in the real estate investing market. Prehabbing means to clear the slate for rehabbers which will buy and hold investment properties as rentals.

It helps in making the properties more appealing and easier for the end buyer. Consecutively, this assists in increasing the perceived value and helps the investor in flipping the houses quickly. Flippers can make use of this strategy to determine a middle ground between wholesaling properties full rehabs and as-is.

For many, this can drastically enhance the property's attractiveness whilst broadening the pool of buyers. In certain scenarios, light rehabbing can transform a rundown property from unlivable to an attractive and functional place for a potential buyer.

As an investor, you would have to determine the amount of improvements needed in the property. A wise way of looking at prehabbing and making it work for you is to view is as:

- A means of maximizing the profit and value of the investing opportunity.
- Ensuring that the time, risks, and improvements involved are minimum.

The main reason most of the real estate investors engage in prehabbing is that most of the potential buyers aren't able to see any potential in the property or perceive a lot of expense and work than there actually is.

There are many cheap houses that are purchased by wholesalers nowadays which are actually in really bad shapes. However, once they have it fixed up, it dramatically changes the property and enhances its value. Once the property is finished with its repairs, you can either sell it immediately or use it as a rental so that you can earn a steady monthly income through it.

28. Lease Options

Lease option is a great way of getting started with real estate investing, particularly when you have little to no cash. It offers you an opportunity of controlling the property without buying it. In this strategy, instead of purchasing the property, you lease it with an option of buying. The lease option contract of real estate is a combination of two main documents – lease and option.

The lease document is in which the owner agrees in letting you lease the property whilst you keep paying the rent till the specified period of time. Throughout the lease duration, the rent can't be increased by the owner, nor can the owner sell or rent out the property to anyone else.

The option document is the indication that you have purchased the right of buying the property in the future, in a certain price. In case you opt for the option of purchasing the property, the owner will have to sell it to you at the decided price.

This part of the contract binds the owner in selling you the property in the option period, but it doesn't put any obligation on you to buy it. The only obligation you have is to make rental payments as per the agreed terms.

If the contract of this strategy is properly structured and written, it offers numerous benefits to the investor. Furthermore, if the contract includes "right to sub-lease" option, then you can even rent out the property and generate a steady cash flow throughout the lease duration.

29. Hard Money Lender

This strategy is usually utilized to finance projects that are exceptionally great deals or when there is a great need of quick money. Usually hard money lenders lend about 50% to 70% of the property's value irrespective of the sales price and close the loans within 2 to 7 days.

Hard money lenders usually overlook the income and credit scores, but they might inquire about the exit strategy or business plan for a project. Hard money can be utilized by investors as a short term funding solution for the real estate deals. You can use this strategy to buy a rental property or fund fix and flips till you can arrange long term financing.

30. Land Trust

Land trust is the least understood strategy yet the most talked about one among the investors. It has traditionally been utilized as a non-profit entity for owning the property. In recent years, there have been many companies that have created methodologies allowing for land trusts to be utilized for acquiring foreclosed properties which enabled homeowners to save their homes and enabled investors to earn great returns.

Land trusts offer easier transactions.

Some also believe land trusts provide the advantage of preventing due-on-sale clauses to force the subject property's refinancing. However, this only happens if the borrower remains the beneficiary of trust and doesn't relate to a transfer of rights of property's occupancy.

CHAPTER 3: EXIT STRATEGY

The successful real estate investors realize the importance of an efficient business model. Developing a proven plan or system enhances the potential of boosting any business towards the forefront of its market.

Hence, both personal development and monetary gains can exponentially also increase through the implementation of a well-designed strategy. This also indicated that the significance of exit strategies can't be underestimated as they are a vital part of a successful strategy.

The investors who take out some time in order to familiarize themselves with the particulars of all processes are always rewarded accordingly. On the contrary, the ones who neglect acknowledging the advantages and importance of having an appropriate exit strategy might be voided of the opportunities of achieving relevance in their industry. It is ultimately up to the investor to establish their success.

Real estate exit strategies are the strategies that help the investors to remove themselves from a real estate deal. Implementation of the right exit strategy is essential for success as the right method results in maximizing their profits and minimizing the risks.

Importance of an Exit Strategy

In many cases, the investors fail in realizing the importance of a proper real estate exit strategy. As a result, they end up losing a lot of time and money in being stuck in deals that aren't profitable.

It is indeed true that implementation speed is rather important when an investor wants to facilitate a transaction; however, it is unwise to start a real estate deal without analyzing the possible exit strategies in order to protect yourself.

To become a successful investor, it is essential that you evaluate all possible scenarios by keeping its end in your mind. This means, that having a certain plan for all the real estate investing deals before you opt for them. You must have a clear idea about which strategy you want to use and how it can benefit you the most.

You must also familiarize yourself with all possible exit strategies that can protect you and save your business from suffering from massive losses. Many investors have lost millions of dollars only because they failed to give much importance to exit strategies.

This can even cost you your real estate investing career. It is reckless to knowingly enter negotiations without determining how you will be able to successfully exit that deal.

Such blind ambition enhances risks but also eliminate potential chances of negotiating from a position of power. It also decreases the potential profits while enhancing the risks.

Influential Factors

The decision of determining the right real estate exit strategy to utilize isn't as simple as it might seem. There are many major factors that must be considered when you plan an exit strategy.

Eventually, the probable profitability of every deal is correlated to the particular chosen strategy. Proper understandings of every plan can assist investors in maximizing the returns on their investments.

However, there isn't any golden rule differentiating between all strategies for a single scenario. Hence, determining which exit strategy to implement depends on the investor's understandings of the following influential factors:

- Property Location
- Profit potential
- Financing options
- Demand and supply
- Property condition
- Property value
- Terms
- Purchase price
- Time to close
- Market conditions
- Level of experience

- Long and short term goals

Knowledge about all these influential factors can help the investors in determining which real estate exit must be used on the particular scenario.

Factors That Ruins an Exit Strategy

Even though, real estate investing is a sound opportunity of making tons of money, there are many risks involved as well which must be taken into consideration by all investors. There are certain factors that can even ruin an exit strategy if the investors aren't careful. Following are some of those factors:

- Depreciation
- Poor management of property that results in reducing its value and hurting the cash flow
- Unpredicted maintenance costs which can drastically reduce or even cancel out the profit
- Lack in demand, lender backing out, or failed escrow prevents a property to get flipped
- Issues with tenants that results in lost rent

Understanding the major factors that might prevent an exit strategy being a success is essential to investors. Successful investors know the right ways of counteracting such obstacles with various strategies.

It is important to have a backup plan as anything can happen in a single moment. Having different exit strategies further lowers the impending risks and enables the investors to earn maximum returns.

CHAPTER 4: BEGINNER MISTAKES TO AVOID AND USEFUL TIPS

6 Common Mistakes to Avoid

Real estate investing is indeed a great means of earning money and is especially rather appealing when the real estate market starts rebounding. However, when beginner investors enters this career, there are bound to be many mistakes which they will make and suffer losses.

Experiencing losses or bad deals can be a huge discouragement in the initial stage of the career. Many even leave this lucrative business when they make mistakes and suffer losses. To avoid all that, here are some of the most common mistakes that all beginner investors make:

1. Believing You Will "Get Rich Quick"

This type of thinking is usually generated by watching those "self-appointed gurus" who appear in infomercials and indicate that apparently it is rather simple to get rich in real estate market.

The truth is, even though you would earn plenty of money, the process isn't simple. There is a lot of effort and hard work involved in this market. You must have proper knowledge and understanding about the strategies and procedures of real estate investing.

You must be smart enough, willing to put in hard work, and also have a good risk tolerance to make it big in real estate investing.

2. Paying a Lot

Another major mistake the beginner investors make is paying too much. This is the main reason why they aren't able to make much money. The profit usually gets locked in when the investor purchases a property.

If mistakes are made in the analysis, the investor typically pays too much for the property and is shocked later when not enough profit is earned in the end.

3. Not Educating Yourself

You can just read a few articles on the internet and start performing a surgery. It required a great deal of training and education. Similarly, you need proper knowledge and guidance when it comes to investing in real estate.

The main mistake made by many investors is that they don't think much before investing in a property which later results in a loss. It is important to educate yourself before you step into this market.

Read books, articles, research papers; attend seminars and workshops; talk with expert real estate investors; work for top real estate investors to learn from them.

4. Not Researching

Typically, it is important for investors to make a quick move on deals before someone else gets them. However, this surely doesn't mean that you immediately sign a contract without doing any research. This is usually what most of the beginners do.

They avoid doing any due diligence regarding the deals, market conditions, costs, and strategies before making the deal and end up exhausting all their personal savings when they aren't able to sell the property or if the property requires more extensive repairs then they anticipated.

Many times beginner investors purchase a property only on an assumption that it will appreciate while they don't have any information that can substantiate that.

5. Miscalculation of Estimates

This is another common mistake made by beginner investors, especially rehabbers. It is recommended that whatever you have estimate the money and time it will take it is best to at least double it as this save you from future losses and would be able to rent out the property or sell it.

6. Underestimate or Overestimating Cash Flow

This is another common beginner mistake many investors make. If you are opting for the buy and hold strategy and are aiming to rent it out then you require adequate cash flow in order to cover the maintenance costs.

It is important that you do proper research on the property, its location, and the market value before estimating the cash flow. You can also seek advice from experts in this field as this will save you from suffering from losing out on profits.

Before making a deal, it is essential to consider the above mention mistakes in order to prevent yourself from going through bad investing experiences, and earning maximum profits from your investments.

Useful Tips for Beginners

Consider the following useful tips that can help you in successfully moving forward and achieving your goals. These will help you in reducing the risks involved and maximizing the profits you earn:

- Before you invest in rental properties, ensure that you are financially strong. It is important to pay attention to your monthly income and budget and ensure that you have sufficient insurance coverage. Majority of the successful investors in real estate create their investment portfolio by saving money and gradually purchasing properties thought the years.

- Never underestimate the significance of a good credit as the best real estate returns depend on the usage of credit for obtaining leverage to utilize OPM (other people's money).

- It is essential that your initial real estate investment, considered as the best one, is to buy a house you would live in. Real estate is the sole investment that you can rent out or live in to generate income. There is also an opportunity to derive major tax free profits when selling off your primary residence at a high cost than you actually paid for.

- It is wise focusing on residential properties when you start off. These properties are an appealing investment and are far easier to manage, purchase, and understand as compared to other properties. If you are a homeowner then you probably already had some experience in maintaining, purchasing, and locating and ideal residential property. This is the reason it is best to start your real estate investing career from.

- All decisions regarding where to invest initiates by analyzing the overall economic trend of the region. If the locality isn't sound economically then it indicates that there isn't much probability of successful real estate investments.

- It is important to understand that you purchase a future cash flow or income stream for yourself when you purchase an investment property. Whatever amount you pay for a property and its generated cash flow makes a great difference in the success and failure of the investment.

- Avoid relying on the numbers provided by the seller when analyzing the potential of a property. Directly inquire about the history of the property from the seller and ask about the reason they are selling. However, avoid relying on historic operating results that the broker or seller provides you with. It is best to do your own research and come up with your own numbers with the help of professional real estate investors.

Consider all these tips and you will be able to avoid risks and obstacles and successfully earn profit for yourself.

CHAPTER 5: FINAL WORDS

Investing in real estate is a wise decision made by many individuals that lead them to earning millions down the road. Compounded by high employment figures and low interest rates, investing a certain amount of money in real estate is an exciting and profitable idea, *if* you have proper knowledge about the strategies and processes involved.

Reading till the end, you would now have a clear understanding about the basics of real estate investing, the processes involved, and ways of earning profits by utilizing the top strategies in real estate investment, which can help you in making a lifetime of wealth and achieve financial freedom.

Now that you are well equipped with the 30 best strategies of real estate investing, it is time to step into the world of real estate investments. You can earn a fortune through real estate investing by using the strategies and other information offered in this book.

ABOUT THE AUTHOR

Michael Joshua got his undergraduate degree in Finance and works full time at a large bank as a Financial Analyst. He has great knowledge in business & money, along with politics and technology.

Goodreads:
https://www.goodreads.com/user/show/46377085-michael-joshua

Twitter:
https://twitter.com/mjoshua_author